The White Valentine

THE WHITE VALENTINE

Mary Woodward

to Anne
with best wishes
Mary
March 2014

First published in 2014 by
Worple Press
Achill Sound, 2b Dry Hill Road
Tonbridge
Kent TN9 1LX.
www.worplepress.co.uk

Cover image by Charlotte Chisholm

Printed by imprintdigital
Upton Pyne, Exeter
www.imprintdigital.net

Typeset by narrator
www.narrator.me.uk
enquiries@narrator.me.uk

ISBN: 978-1-905208-22-7

Acknowledgements

Thanks to the following publications in which some of these poems first appeared: *Ambit, Jewish Quarterly, the London magazine, the North, Poetry Ireland, THE SHOp, Stand, the Times newspaper.*

'The Hills of Tinnacara' was a runner up in the National Poetry competion1996, 'Enda's Letter' was a runner up in the Arvon competition in 2005, 'Lodging' was shortlisted for the Strokestown International poetry prize in 2008, 'Autumn at Number Nine' was a runner up in the Troubadour competition in 2010. 'Sweetheart' and 'Cooking with Elizabeth Craig' were respectively longlisted and shortlisted in the Bridport competition in 2006 and 2012. 'Our Ladies' was a runner up in the Yorkshire Open in 2009 and 'Maggie Philomena' was listed in the Fish poetry competition in 2009.

Thanks to Peter Sansom for his long term support, and to him and Michael Laskey for their work on the Poetry Trust seminar in 2008. Thanks also to my colleagues and friends in the Mary Ward workshop, Bloomsbury, and the poets who have worked with us so often, especially Christopher Reid, Hugo Williams and Maurice Riordan.

Of course I may be remembering it all wrong

Elizabeth Bishop

Santarém

Contents

i.m. Morris and Blakey

The Dining Room

She is reading Kropotkin's memoirs at dinner,
after a day's riding, and an early evening walk
through the pines to sit and watch the bay.

Her brother is planning a cricket match;
her father, silent, is remembering summer nights
adrift near Spitsbergen, the Arctic birds
wheeling in the white light, the ship whispering.

The count, her husband, has been painting the walls,
a portrait to each column. Three times life size,
he and Josslyn stare over the table through the oil light.
The butler, the head gardener and the black and white terrier
that follows them around the demesne are there too,
and regard indifferently the porcelain, the half –
finished desserts. Beyond the house
the ocean moves against the forested shore.
In the kitchen the servants plan their own redemptions.

The Schoolroom, Temple House

The schoolroom light pulls down
on a hinged balance, its light

glowing over the table, his bent head
and his notes on Marlborough's

victories. He likes history,
finds it clear and easy to memorise

– plans to take it further and
works hard on this essay. His tutor

is already asleep, the house
quiet. By the lake

the mallards shuffle in the
rushes, men in cord jackets,

young faces covered, move
towards the terrace. They will

leave with the rifles or fire
the place. His essay is nearly

finished when he hears the
glass break, the soft voices.

The Hills of Tinnacara

He was from some Liverpool 7 back street,
      went to a brown brick Board school, where
            he hated mental arithmetic and
      team games; liked going home to a coal fire,
            and to the market on Saturdays, loved Mass on Sundays
in the shadowy church, Latin on the altar, candles, his
                              mum's rosary.
      A church like the one in France, three years back,
            with the same velvety, incense touched
                  dark air,
dark air like that around his eyes now,
            black and deepening. He knew he was lying
                  at the side of
the switchback, rolling lane down the slopes of Tinnacara,
            grass beneath his head and he could smell
                  the petrol seeping out into the road
and just see the shattered armoured car against the night.

There were no English voices anymore, just still shapes
            slumped against the wheel guards
and the soft beautiful accents crossing the darkness high
                              over him
      and his own whispering of 'get me a priest' and one of
                              them
            said clearly, 'this one's taking longer',
and he let his face fall sideways into the gentle moss and
                              wondered
      why it was going to be here,
            here
in the gorse – sweet, pure Irish air, not the foul, crawling
                        French mud.

3

That was the poem I wrote. You might have written another.
    I've made up Liverpool and the French mud, though
        both were possibilities.
What is true is the death,
       the dying man wanting a priest
    and the men who'd blown up the armoured car,
        devout Catholics all, ignoring his last request.

The truth straight from my grandmother who'd tell it years
                              later,
    standing by her little shrine to the Infant Child of Prague,
next to the lace covered window that looked down the
                       front meadow
    and out towards Mullaghroe.
Arra, I can imagine her saying to my mother, briefly at home
    from nursing in the East End during the Blitz,
Arra, Kathleen, wouldn't you have thought they'd have got
    a dying man a priest?
And my mother keeping the story and telling me, though
    not adding whether or not her father was one of them,
        and now in time, the story is yours too,
           one way or the other.

Enda's Letter

Your second letter arrived this week,
green edged air mail. The only place in the world
to have those envelopes, I'll bet,
and in case that's not enough, a small printed
shamrock and Bronze Age jewellery on the stamp,
Tobair an Choir on the post mark: my address
in royal blue. You don't seem too bothered
about countries, England's an afterthought
in the corner. With your own you get as far
as Gurteen but no further. What are
states and nations your writing seems to say?
Four Easter eggs and *holldays* from school,
two kisses and a heart.

Aren't there laws against letters as young
as this travelling on their own by air?
You've only been around five years. Hardly time
to learn to clean your teeth, and here you are
sending a whole page of proper sentences
thousands of miles, getting foreign post codes
right, being taken seriously by postmen,
addressing me as Ms. and, no doubt, by now
learning like a grown up to wait for a reply.

Clooneigh – the meadow of the horses

The horses must have been years and years back;
I can only remember a grazing donkey and
a few black and white Friesians, straight backed,
big and slow and warm in the sun,
rambling down this meadow side of a hill,

sloping to flatter, marshier land, a broken stone wall
and the early reaches of the Owenmore, which
the younger cattle would wade into, screened
by the low lying bushes which once hid the men
who'd blown up the Sligo / Dublin train.

From there, looking up from the wet hoofed grass
the old house seemed small, just a white line
along the lane's hedge, the field itself
broader than the whole farm's length,
maybe four hundred yards across, immense,

starred with yellow bolathorns, a rhombus of land
which could take a whole life or lives to work,
and did, from men who left women and boys
to cope the best they could: so huge it took a man
a week to dig it for seeding, a week of feeding

the children soda bread and milk, and keeping
the eggs and some precious specially bought steak
to give the worker the energy to keep digging.
When my grandfather was old it would shock him
to see that for his town bred grandchildren

it was simply a playground, to be rolled down, run up;
he'd lean his bike by the top wall and hand over silver rolls
of mints he'd bought with the porter in the shop
two miles away, almost tell them to stop but didn't.
It belonged to so many, all the generations fed from it,

and fled from it, who dreamed homesick dreams of it
that went on and on for a century an ocean away,
who took August holiday snapshots of it, from the top, across,
looking up; who remembered the countless gallons of water
dragged up it in buckets every morning and evening.

And every early spring it looked as it must have done
the first day it was measured out and walled in,
huge and open and beautiful and difficult,
murmuring, to those who would hear it, once again
its faithful, terrible bargain, care for me and you will live.

Census

The evening of Sunday, the second of April, nineteen eleven,
is falling over the parish of Kilfree where the farms
of the townlands of Cloonanure, Cloontycarn,
Cuilmore, Cuilpruglish, Greyfield, Chacefield,
Moydough, Moygara, Mullaghroe and Seefin
are shutting doors and settling for the night. At home
in Clooneigh the official form kept carefully behind
The Infant Child of Prague is taken down, smoothed out.
A pen is found, and ink. It will take time. Names. Then
religion, profession, length of marriage, children dead and alive.
Literacy and languages to be declared. And then the farm.
The number of outbuildings and their uses, the house, its roof,
whether thatch or tile, the number of doors and windows,
each is counted. It is signed, folded. Back in the envelope.

They are all caught alive in this feather breath moment
of writing: the Stensons, Toolans, Daveys, the Keenans,
the Brennans, the Healeys and the Carrs, and
Bridget Rodgers, sixty nine, single and alone in a one room cottage,
farmer and poultry keeper. They are all farmers,
even the schoolmaster; all Catholic. Everyone over
sixty five, and noone younger, can use Irish.
Fires are quietened, oil lamps put out.

Monday dawned. Cold maybe, or was it an early spring,
an easy morning to rise and start again? Soon the enumerator
will arrive at every house, check the forms, write for those
who cannot. X *'her mark'* puts Bridget. In Clooneigh
my grandfather, still unmarried, the last one left,
and his mother begin the week's work. Ahead is waiting
the terrible patient silent future, a new family, war,
revolution, a young country, phones and planes,
piped water, and electricity brought by blond Germans.

Michael McNulty's bike rattles to a halt.
The form is handed over, put into his care, forgotten. He fits it
in the pannier with all the others, pedals off, heading
for Drimhilloch, swerving to miss the busy chickens in the lane.

The Midnight Returns

There's a whole city burning
to the ground out there. When she last looked,
pulling back a fraction of the blackout
in the Izal scrubbed, patients' bathroom,

there was blazing everywhere. Whitechapel, Aldgate.
Streaming searchlights for the anti-aircraft guns
booming from Hackney Marshes,
the sergeants' voices calling Fire in her mind.

The ward is silent; too sick to go to the shelters
these sleep out the raid, or pretend to,
each bed a little cave of safe darkness
in the night lamps' gentian shadow.

She begins the midnight returns,
white cuff moving across the ward ledger,
pen accounting for each still, breathing body,
initials the careful list, dates it.

There'd be none of this back home,
no bombs, no incendiaries there –
Their farm unthreatened, the Atlantic sky
an infinite meadow of free and tranquil stars,

drowsy black and white cows warm in the shed,
hooves smelling of the Owenmore's mud.
She closes the ward book, glances at her watch.
All medication done, temperatures checked.

Fire engines, now, screaming close by, frantic.
She prays, of course, mother of god, protect us,
touching the little ripple of her rosary
in the pocket of her navy dress;

knows nothing promises them even another minute;
each circle of her watch hand a victory,
willing their journey to the morning,
to the shrapnel covered pavements, singed pigeons,

the early buses starting up the day.

The Hard Stuff

A pub, a summer evening,
a friend orders a glass of Jamesons.
The smell makes me homesick,
the soft smoky sheen on the air.

My grandmother, old, ill
in the dark farmhouse bedroom,
a world where there's
no Nurofen, no doctors, no NHS helpline,
holding a miniature of whiskey.

My dad still at home on the day
he died, managing to laugh
when I suggested a Catholic hot toddy.
His last ever drink.

Just the smell makes me homesick,
comforting, aromatic; all you need
to face the hard stuff.

Our Ladies

Three days to go, early January,
I work too fast to let myself think.
Post-It notes on each bin-liner:
out/ flat/ Oxfam. Tablecloths, napkins,
towels, sheets, ornaments, china, cutlery;
all edited and filed. Pictures, books,
purses with out-of-date stamps in,
old writing cases, long ago reading glasses:
childhood meditations, the very things of life,
culled and gone.
And now and then another of these,
clear plastic, five inches high,
Lourdes or Knock or Walsingham, on their faces
in the socks, or leaning sideways in the cleaning basket,
or upright in the cupboard under the sink
next to the new block of Fairy soap.
You can't need so many, I say, Goneril-like,
wondering whether in this case out means Oxfam,
or really Out. I already feel guilty enough
about the Holy Water which I've been pouring
on the plants. But in the end they are all gone. Out.
Hands clasped, eyes still demurely fixed on heaven.

I move on, to the garden shed, clear the deckchairs,
check the garage, then in the greenhouse
my foot strikes something in the patch of earth.
where the tomatoes used to grow: face down, half buried,
on a grander scale, a foot high, flowing robes,
crowned, another Our Lady of Walsingham
at last defeated in this vale of tears,
water pointlessly sloshing around inside her.

Regina Coeli. Stella Maris. Queen of Loss.

Maggie Philomena

She's getting nearer these days,
creeping along the icy damp corridor
after me, hectic flush on her cheeks

doing little to disguise the wax white
complexion. Like a statue, a scapular,
but holier because she's real

or was, before she took it into her head
to go into the convent, a place
as cold as the winter sea,

and filthy with tubercular coughs
and sneezes. Microbes waited, pious
in the cuffs of her habit, when she lifted

her hands to pray. And there was
no end of that: morning, noon and night
the few months she was there

before she died, only eighteen, lone blue eyes
among seven brown eyed siblings.
Then this holy name to be handed down;

not her first, real life name, but some
catacomb martyr virgin who turned out
never to have existed. Passed on

to encourage a child to death.
Remember her. Mind these lessons:
Be silent. Be good. Be nothing.

War Wedding

I know for a fact what didn't happen after:
you didn't come back. That was your last,
your final leave. You didn't move from Cardigan
to London after the war. Didn't marry a sharp-tongued,
pretty Shepherd's Bush girl. Didn't father
a set of cousins living just down the road,
William and Vic and Alice and Rachel and Hannah,
the cousins who didn't grow up with my dad,
going swimming together in the baths in Lime Grove,
who weren't there for Christmases,
and the pub, and the park. You're like the butterfly
in that sci-fi story: your destruction hardly noticed
but, for all I know, if you'd lived
everything might've been different, better, even for me.

Your few, counted days home before Gallipoli;
you are, I'd bet from your stance, the best man;
with a magnifying glass (yes, I've bothered to do this)
your sergeant's stripes are just visible.
Your big left hand is on my grandmother's shoulder,
your new sister-in-law, proud, firm on the good wool
of her quietly fashionable winter suit. Only twenty two,
under the Welsh Regiment cap and badge,
you have the long wise weary face of an old horse,
sad as if it's all already happened:
the long journey, the struggles with your kit,
the men, ending up somewhere never even mentioned
in the geography you did at school.
Never mind not Welsh, not even the Empire.

Your expression is both soldierly and somehow aghast
as if in that moment when the camera clicked
you realised that was it, was all you'd leave us.
Nonsense to believe love is stronger than death,
but something is – anger or the persistence of a life.

The '36 Olympics

Bronze

The little boy with wet hair and chattering teeth, striped towel
under one arm, waits at the door, looking out into Marshall Street.
Behind him he can still hear the echoes in the warm chlorine-
                                                    heavy air.
He is waiting for his father, the lifeguard, to finish his shift,
                                                    change, give in
his keys and then they will walk up to Oxford Street for the bus
                                                    home.
He will talk all the way, his brown fringe spiky with damp,
and he will ask again and again 'Was it any good? Was that dive
fast enough? Straight enough? Am I good?' on and on, at the
                                                    bus top,
then over the changing gears, his head still swimming
with the hurtling, curling fall into the blue, the green water.

Silver

Another war over and done with, and a different swimming pool,
West London this time, and a day out, coach drawn up waiting,
the whole swimming club lined up for a photo, grinning, young,
and he's there, towel under elbow, fag in mouth,
maybe just beginning to think all this was a bit much…
all this training, all this effort, with two young kids
and a job with the Electricity Board adding up figures all week.
And his own father getting too old to nag him much
any more about timing this somersault or that,
and when he hits the water now that old feeling
of spiralling flight becoming… not dull but less of a miracle.

Gold

…summer seashores and he'd dive in from the shallows, head
straight for the horizon so fast we'd get frightened and panic
and run around on the beach yelling 'come back, come back'.
He got slower, of course; the silver cups increasingly inexplicable
but the old club racing shorts, faded to a watery blur, never replaced.

His favourite swimming tale, always told with a wave of a lit
                                                    cigarette,
wasn't about a win of his own: how his team mate Bert Thomas,
picked for the Berlin Olympics, stopped a shirted, belted
                                        Storm trooper
in the Friedrich Strasse '*Good uniform, mate – bus conductor, are you?*'
was arrested, rescued from unamused Nazi bureaucrats by
                                        British officials…

a Londoner's little story retold often, long after the high diving
                                                    boards,
the split second timing, the light spinning itself into the blue
                                                    green water
had become so distant it must have seemed those had only ever
                                                    been part
of the little boy at the door of the swimming pool, waiting to
                                        go home.

Transfer

He'll be blue-lighted across London , says the nurse.
Then sees our faces. Adds *with a doctor.* At night,
We hope, calculating the time it will take:
Out of Camberwell, up to Waterloo Bridge,
Past St Paul's, through the stony sleeping city,
Into Whitechapel. Brakes, the doors opening.
Minutes, maybe only minutes, if the way is clear
Away from this safe cave of screens and tubes
To another sleepless factory for saving lives.
Blue lighted as if to warn off Pluto's scouts.
That, and the siren, protective. Echoing straight through
Stilled junctions, cars huddling up to kerbs for this driver
Who owns the roads like his or her own arteries,
Uniformed, anonymous, and the blue light
Turning, burning; all of us thinking fight, fight.

The Boating Lake

Without preliminary stutters or hesitations
the engine stops. The new silence encloses us
glassily while the little boat sways, disconcerted,

without motivation or purpose. The soft smell
of petrol expands around me. I might be
only four but I know this shouldn't have

happened. We should still be going round
the lake in our pointless, enjoyable circles. I don't
in fact know much about anything, but I do also

know I can't swim. That won't happen for
another three years till one hot summer in Mill Hill
outdoor pool when I manage to take my feet off

the bottom. But my feet are not on the bottom here;
this bottom is probably quite a long way away
from the cold glossy dark green around us.

There is noone near. Even my careful mother, on
whom I can usually rely, is busy on the distant bank
with my little brother and my cousin. I don't mean

to, but I am overcome with tears. *Don't cry,*
says my aunt, *Don't cry*, pulling desperately
at the little wheel with no scrap of effect on the boat,

the nose of which is turning round and round,
is become a corkscrew which will bore its way down
and down and down to the dead ducks, the tangly weeds

and lost balls underneath us. Maybe I will suddenly
possess the power to strike up and swim like
Deep Sea Mokey, the donkey in my book, who lives

with the shrimps and sea creatures, and seems
quite at ease with them all. But I am far from convinced.
I am still crying and my aunt is waving wildly;

then a man in a bigger boat is next to us, reaches over
and pulls at something beneath our helm.
The lawnmower noises start up again. We resume

our circles. I stop crying. But I am a different child.

Google Streetview

In the black void between Boxing Day and New Year
I pass the hours Google Streetviewing all the addresses
I send Christmas cards to that I've never visited: old aunts,
second cousins, friends from way back. Houses, tidy bungalows
and flats all as I imagined them, in quiet streets I arrow up

and down, sometimes passing summer gangs of children playing
on the kerbs of pavements I've never walked. Then I Streetview
my own address, raking along all the parked cars till I find
my old Ford, long since scrapped, still loyal in my favourite place
where I always imagined it was less likely to be bumped.

I zoom in by the lamp-post near which Mosey used to sit
purring in the sun but I don't really want to find him;
he's been dead six months; I don't want him trapped, silent
in the Ever-Forever Land Of Google Streetview where
I can't call him and see him run towards me. So I set off

hundreds of miles and Google Streetview the old house
where we had a flat when first married, the flat with the balcony
and the pretty urban view through the boulevard of trees,
across to the busy road with the deli, where we used to buy
salami and poppy seed cake. But the shops, all of them,

are boarded up with metal sheets, block after block,
as if there has been a war. Some war I heard of distantly
but until now failed to realise the horror of. Numb, I decide
to revisit the house where everything went wrong, and find it,
innocent enough in the digital light, though the front lawn

is now concrete, and the pub nearby looks hostile, the weeds
in the car park issuing warnings I did not hear then.
Exhausted, I see no point in holding back from tracking down
that country lane you used to live along, to find your house,
charming, rural, almost hidden by thorn trees, quite unlike the

block of flats where you live now. *Where I think you live now.*
Maybe you don't. This is the Land of Not Quite True after all.
I magnify the entrance but there are no clues, What did I hope for
anyway? Your face at a window? You, coming out the door
to walk along the street in that way I'll never forget?

The Moon Landing

It didn't bother us that it was shown at 3 in the morning.
Early hours were routine; all those late nights of meeting up

in the Phil or the Grapes, and then a meal at the Yuet Ben,
the big shared bowl of soup probably, with the green leaves

and garlic, and then after jasmine tea and toffee bananas
we'd walk back for cards and coffee in Denby Arabesque

cups, and more drinking, maybe wine or Guinness
and blackcurrant. The flat, that Sunnyside flat, was white

throughout, all the furniture painted silver, even the piano.
A world quite moonlike in itself. And we watched

in black and white, and we weren't even that impressed.
We knew things were moving forward. Getting better.

The moon? The stars? We were astronauts too.

The White Valentine

This year, at last, I could send you a valentine –
a white card in a white envelope, your name
and address stuck on in crooked, cut out letters;
but don't worry, there's no ransom note inside.
I have nothing to bargain with or for, nothing.

Your bewilderment will increase as you pull out
the folded card – empty, unmarked,
off white watercolour paper,
rough edges as if torn by hand, the fold
scored with a bone bookmaker's tool. Almost
a work of art in its blankness and lack.

You'll turn it over, hold it up to the light.
Nothing. You'll look at the envelope again.
Postmarked Central London, though I have considered
going to Paris to post it. Almost any city
would have done: Oslo, Anchorage, Helsinki – somewhere
still deep in snow would have been suitable.
A cold gift, a white valentine from a winter place
heart-high in ice, where they speak another language
and the flights out are grounded.

You might throw it away. Or slip it
in one of your books, think about it now and then.
You will never know who sent it. No point even trying to guess.
I vanished from your life so long ago even the idea of youth
is beyond thaw; your name in my old diary hangs
dangerously in a fragile icicle of memory,
this uncreated card as perfect as everything that didn't happen

Sweet Heart

The Big Issue seller on the corner
where Bruton Street joins Bond Street
calls me sweetheart,
and the West Indian man in Pageant Road
on New Year's Eve, when he was out videoing
his Christmas house lights,
the ones with Santa Claus pedalling a bike,
said sweetheart too.
And I think yeah in my dreams do I have
a sweet heart, know what there is
in the catarrhal dark of my chest
has now no claim to sweetness
but, stubborn, the epithet carries
the optimistic gold and scarlet loveliness
of Middle English, or a Tudor lyric.

Sweet heart; and like everyone
once upon a time so I was
sweet hearted, a sweetheart,
walked hand in hand in the street,
was bought flowers,
thought love was, like air or water,
our element.

Sweet heart, noun and qualifier
tagged so lightly
to the quotidian, adrift on the hours,
handed out as if hearts were

mille feuilles

or choc ices

or macaroons,

but for a second, in the saying of
so it becomes, for that second,
on city corner or night time street.

Risotto

I'd work from recipes, measure carefully, hover
anxiously. Be so bored by the craft and science
I'd then lose all interest in eating it.
So I cooked risotto every night for a month,
made it instinctive, natural, a simple habit,
as if I'd grown up in a red tiled Italian town
where emerald basil sprouts wildly in the gutters.

Rice, onion, garlic abandoned into hot butter
without a thought. Pepper. Bubbling white wine.
Stock, slipping from a jug uncalculated.
Dared break the cardinal rule never to leave it.
Judged by eye. Knew by the soft heaving gloss
when to let saffron or prawns or asparagus
fall from my heedless hands. Got it so perfect

I can start from scratch, soon be piling plates,
like breathing, like walking, like humming Puccini,
as if another woman, olive eyed, laughing
like Sunday church bells all the while, has done it.

Cooking with Elizabeth Craig

Linen cover intact but, first pages gone,
it opens at p.8 with sepia pictures,
How I Save Money in the Kitchen:

odds and ends of cheese make savouries;
the peelings from an apple pie make jelly.
Mostly pristine through Choose and Store

and Things You Want to Know,
though on p.27 a big pencilled pram
reaches from header to footer

over How to Fold, Knead and Marinate,
and How to Mix Mustard. Only
odd squiggles through the Up-to-Date

Kitchen, Breakfast Dishes, until Sweet
Sauces, Cold and Hot, whereupon
a strange bug-eyed creature, pencil

again, straddles from spine to
margin. Assorted motifs and curves
in Luncheon and Supper Snacks,

dolls' beds at the end, beneath Corned
Beef Hash and Bubble and Squeak.
By p.79 almost Celtic curlicues under

To Garnish Fish Cutlets. Later in the text
thick dark brown crayon scrolled
over Steak and Kidney Pie and Veal Patties.

Poultry, too, is a busy chapter: a second
creature, beyond any guess at species,
obliterates Roast Chicken and Boiled

Fowl. Another pram supports Creamed
Haddock. But the heart of the work is to be
found where 98 and 99 fall apart: paper

yellowed with use, several prams and dashing
lines adorn Cream of Split Pea soup, the soup
of soups, that could bring the dead to life.

City of Change and Challenge

hoped the blurred postmarks on letters sent home
all those aching mornings or evenings
from old VR post boxes on the corners of streets
where a faithful worn-out past came and went.
Buses were oddly green. Even the sky had shifted.

Two pounds a week from the bank
in Great Charlotte Street, till they knocked it down;
then Church Street, still from the same cashier,
nearly sixty, a rose in his buttonhole,
courteous, dignified, even though all around him
his city was yet again roaring, falling
rubble, a chaos of high-piled broken walls.

Acres of destruction. Holes; this city was full of holes,
a great pink sandstone cheese. In dark back terraces
butcher shops were selling trays of pig tails.
Buying my own toothpaste in Boots I felt as cast off
as Robinson Crusoe. At night tugs hooted heartbreakingly

in the foggy estuary, melancholy and insistent
as if they too were far from home, longed
to put on speed, and just sail off out of there.
Back. Back. Back where peace was safely hire-purchased,
where the Blitz had been neatly tidied up.
Here the war was hanging on, derelict, desperate
to remain, to be allowed to rest, to be left alone.

I'd run away from Keats and Blake down the hill,
wander around the big shops like a stray lost pet,
hoping a sense of safety might surface
in some sniff of normality in Lewis's aisles,
or C & A's, or Marks and Spencer; eking out

my two pounds from the man with the rose in his lapel
whose home, after all, this was. The roses,
the way he'd bothered with the roses, helped.

Lodging

A double bass stood, unused but often admired,
in the corner, a mute reminder of the crane driving

public-school educated jazz musician husband
who'd recently hanged himself in Symondshyde Wood.

The place teemed with rescued, sulky cats, and small boys
rushing and shrieking like young midshipmen in a force ten gale.

Poland filled the house with a brooding medieval winter.
Myths of destitute fathers selling rags from barrows

making enough money to take on the middle class
were brandished as proof noone ever needed to vote Labour.

There were cream and jam-marbled Napoleonskis at Daquise's,
crowded with Catholic priests and old ladies in veiled hats.

At Easter sorrel soup, with new potatoes, hard boiled eggs,
welcomed the spring still so slow in coming.

I'd walk to work hours early in search of normality:
two miles in ankle-wrenching high wedge heels.

One evening the children hanged a teddy bear
from their bedroom window. The strangest of the cats

took to the top of my wardrobe, a tabby basilisk
refusing all offered strokes, invitations to friendship.

I packed my Penguin Guide to English Literature and left,
weighing six stone despite all the poppy seed cake.

Dickins and Jones 2006

The last things are sold, terminal transactions
of a hundred and twenty years of ringing tills,

warm silver and copper, cheques, credit cards,
ceremonies of white paper and monogrammed bag

now all done, though the bronze name plates
remain at the side of the doors; the row of faded

union jacks hangs lifeless in the leaden winter
air, vibrato of the Regent Street traffic failing

to raise an answering tremor in the thin fabric.
In Liberty's, the ground floor between Guerlain

and Balmain, the tall dark boy (who sold me
Shalimar the weekend after the bombs) says

to his colleague *They've stripped everything…*
look in at the edges of the windows. Everything.

Not the columns, I hope, not the rotunda, not yet,
the last grand magasin we had, once the others lost

themselves in a frenzy of retail reinvention,
LED lighting, and scary escalators; nowhere

now with the dark, sinuous enticement Zola pinned
down in *Au Bonheur des Dames*, nowhere left

where you trail up after veiled hats, narrow gloves,
silk stockings, or stand next to gauzy handkerchief-

hemmed summer dresses in the wobbly lift, to a cafe
where friends would meet every week for fifty years.

Decades gone, all gone, the serenity of it, the halls
I dawdled through my first summer of being single,

finally with money to spend on myself. Now my only
relic the dark rose, sequinned scarf kept in its icy tissue,

the one I'd throw across my desk before a full day's
teaching, to remind me life still had things to offer.

The V&A: evening dresses

Schiaparelli 1953
pale pink organza, embroidery,
under-dress of Thai silk;

Balenciaga 1955
scarlet silk taffeta, wired flounces,
on a boned and padded foundation;

Jacques Heim 1959
dark rose silk organza,
under-dress of silk taffeta;

evening dresses, not to be seen before eight,
which swayed and danced and circled
at parties or receptions, in rooms misty
with tobacco, rooms full of people still
finding it hard to believe the war was over,
that peace seemed to be lasting,
though maybe only just, while the Cold War
was there every morning in the headlines
like a knife held to their ribs;
dresses for which Edmundo Ros
or Stephane Grappelli were as hot as it got;
unimaginable grown up evenings which went on
while I was spending my time drawing
ladies' dresses, only seen in films and magazines,
dresses full of the panache and serious glamour
little girls know is more real life
than the sensible skirts and tops
which pass them in school or on the street;
dresses which are now museum pieces,
their wearers lolling in wheelchairs or dead,
slender waists and arms just memories

for the middle-aged rich children
who kissed them goodnight in a valedictory cloud
of L'Air du Temps or Ma Griffe, who too
had thought they looked like princesses.

Baudelaire, at sea

All down the coast of Africa he sulks.
This is not his idea; he would not have left Paris
for a day, let alone these weeks in a cabin
too small for stretching out comfortably.
He has read his complete Balzac, and the other passengers,
four of them, are as dull as the crew.
Boredom consumes him. He is so tired of it:
the ocean, the vast sky, the distances,
the god-awful emptiness of nature.
Silent, he sits on deck, drawing in a notebook,
small sketches of the rigging, the rails, the lifeboat.
and wonders who is writing what at home.

Rounding Cape Horn a storm as irritable as he is
rescues him from this ennui; day and night it seethes,
grumbles, whinges round them, then goes too far –
he recognises the pattern – and snaps the mast.
With one despairing roll the ship is on her side.
He closes his notebook and joins the yelling sailors,
pushes up his linen sleeves and grabs a corner
of tar-coated canvas. Better even this
than never see Paris again. For the only time
in his life part of a team, he wrenches
and pulls until somehow they coax and urge
the prélart to rise, swell, and right the vessel.

That is it. Enough now of all the silly talk
of the Orient, and travel, and seeing the world.
He has his own adventure to pursue.
When the ship docks at Reunion he clambers down
the ladder, Collected Balzac hugged in his arms,
drenched by twelve foot waves. He wants his life back,
wants his city, the little streets, the rivals,

the bars, the talk. The captain writes
to the general, his stepfather, to warn him
Charles is coming back. *His mind was set.*

The Sea Deer

Excited gulls diving make him bring the boat over
thinking that this means mackerel though

the streaked silver in the water coming closer
is not scales shimmering but a young roebuck,

head sparkling with a falling coronet of sea water,
swimming out here a quarter mile from land,

snatched and stolen by some rustling tide, hoofs circling wildly now
in the brown darkness that parts and parts beneath ...

It is the effort

of a lifetime to lean over the side and down
and to grab the bobbing antlers and quivering neck

and to haul

the deer, only half grown but still summer sturdy,
in, bewildered, gilded and sticky with salt water,

to lie there, the unlikeliest catch, catching his breath,
watching the man turn the boat from the impossible horizon

catching his breath and waiting, waiting for the trees
to begin again, to have around him the bracken and the brambles,

dry summer grass smelling of daylight

and the air clean with the silences of his knowledge
and the earth fixed still beneath him.

The Portuguese Storm

Though it's not even evening yet
it's black out there. The air is
swelling with water and sometime soon,
in an hour, maybe two – from off the coast of Portugal
the storm will have arrived. The little rivers hereabouts
will recall their real natures, rise to their banks
and level out with the meadows.

I am marking test papers and my big black and white cat
is with me, lying happily in the lamplight while the loose
gutter next door drips noises over
the steady drip of the rain. I stop for a moment,
irritated, wishing my neighbours would fix it.

Then the tape I am playing stops and here, within, it is silent
though by midnight the real wildness will be upon us.

Tomorrow I will have to drive to work through floods again.
The fields will have crawled yellow into and through their hedges.

The forest pond near Well End will have taken over the road
and there will be wetness everywhere and
little lanes will stretch like narrow lakes.
With you it feels the same: I used to know this way
but it's become unrecognisable, the ground is breaking up,
only good guesswork will tell me if I am in too deep,
my fingers crossed that the brakes still work.

Cy Twombly's Hero and Leandro

True love is mute and oft amazed stands.
Thus while dumb signs their yielding hearts entangled
The air with living sparks was spangled

Polyptych: green and rose water lashes, jumping,
across canvases, threatens to drench and
wipe out the last moments of Keats' sonnet,
up bubbles his amorous breath.

Brings back the story; in Marlowe's version
the most erotic poem in the English language
so we were told in a lecture. I read it that evening.

Hero, reluctant, is persuaded. Her lover
though determined, persistent, perishes
in the winter sea, her guiding light become
too small, useless. Once it touched me
how they died, he defeated, she despairing;
love's holy fire no more than sodden ashes
on the salty shingle. But no, it's not the sea,
not Twombly's rushing, beautiful waters
which do for love. Girls give in and wait.
Signal faithfully through the dark nights.
To lovers who drown right enough but
in the crashing swell of their own selves,
fade off, gurgling, become forgotten flotsam.

Why the English like Jack Vettriano's Singing Butler

It's got stormy weather, a lowering mauve grey sky
and a mean looking tide creeping away in the distance.

A puddly beach. Could be Southport or Frinton.
You can almost feel the shivers in your still damp socks.

It's got a couple: a woman not in the first flush of youth
with a big bum and a Very Red Dress from a local shop,

and a man, maybe a lover but more likely her husband,
who thought, after two gins, this might be a good way

to liven up their twenty fifth anniversary lunch,
and has been regretting it for the last ten minutes.
Now he just feels daft. And his shoes are ruined.

And it's got Servants: Olive the maid, who has an
interview soon for a better job, in a stocking factory,
folding the pairs together and putting them flat in
cellophane packets. More money. Weekends off.

And Arthur, Somme survivor, who's planning
to move to London and find a place with people
with old money, big dogs, and no half-baked
bloody silly notions picked up from the pictures.

Autumn at Number Nine

The 'decorating' is over now, the hammers silent.
A pile of ragged old russet carpet out the front
speaks of effort as it sits lumpily heaped
near the broken microwave and the shelf fittings,

by the recycling box, open to the rain, full of
liquid food supplement bottles, the stuff
Nana is kept alive by, just about, handed to her
by her grandson while his margherita pizzas,

from Iceland, nice with a Stella (those
cans thrown in there too), are heating up.
Out the back a layered pyramid of rusty timbers,
plastic sheeting, cycle frames, old cat litter trays

is climbing the back fence. The barbecue,
a little crooked, is to one side, not touched
since things erupted with Gary the lodger that hot
Sunday lunchtime, but maybe it'll be handy

next summer. Left over from this one,
the green plastic chairs sit splayed in the rain,
full of the ghosts of the mates who used
to come here for a get-together and a bit of rap

back when the shed was wired for sound.
Back before the neighbours got awkward
and the council started to come on heavy. Yeah,
it was good then, a laugh, when his mum

was still alive but, only forty six, she passed
away in June, so quick, in the Royal Free. It isn't
the same without her but the funeral went ok. Forget
that spot of trouble after, when he was out

the front with Gary, and Jade'd popped round
to sympathise; and the wheelie bin was sideways
for them to sit on when a sarky bloke with leaflets
asked for the sharp end of Jadie's tongue.

How could they know he was a Lib Dem councillor?
No, it's too quiet without mum around. And after all
that's happened, the things which made life worth living,
a drink, a cigarette, have turned out not to be

such good friends after all. They've learned that much,
him and his nan. You can't rely on anything really.
Now the music's had to stop, it's dead. But the days pass
by all right, the numbered days till Nana goes off too.

The Summer of the Killer Frogs

It was just so hot, day after day,
and London was like a southern European city
smelling of perfume and stale drains,
brown shoulders and legs gleaming
                everywhere as if the
                        West End was one big beach;

every evening I had pasta and one glass of wine
                in the same cafe;
every night I went home to watch
                the terrible news,
terrified people leaving their villages and animals
                and driving to nowhere,
                        stones through windscreens.

Every night too warm to sleep and when I did
                I'd always dream of him,
                        not even of him – just of
                                looking for him, dreaming of his absence.

It was just so hot, day after day,
                like southern Europe,
and the evening paper kept printing accounts
                of huge frogs in London ponds –
                        cannibals, eating ordinary frogs
                        in one go.

Each evening there'd be another picture.
I'd eat my ravioli, the noise of Old Compton Street
                yelling outside the cafe,
and look at these frogs with their huge round eyes
                like big pebbles,

then struggle back on a shimmering train
    through glowing suburbs and yellow fields
to another night of watching war and then
    endless dreams of how I could not have him.

The Empire of Evil 1983

Me, a coach load of Swedish tourists
and a magician from New York

in a Leningrad so gilded
by August it seemed a city

from another version of history:
no snow, no furs, no bells.

Nor had we expected to be so free.
The magician would take a tram
each day to explore the suburbs
of tower blocks, and do card tricks
for the people in the streets.

Jeez, he said, *it's all so ordinary,*
just everyone walking their dogs.

Sachsenhausen

First, baby shoes:

all those bones in such a little space, room just
enough to fit in a finger. Strap
just long enough to button
round an egg. Leather to get hard with years
walked away in others.

Shoes give away

whatever you know about who you are
and where you are going. Early on
choices are made for you: silent,
sullen, test foot laced in to what you didn't want,
every step a lie. But soon enough they
can't hold you back: red, green, punched, blue,
heeled, little flat bows, patent like new tar.

Sensible shoes for work

for your body, carried by these, has decades
to climb, corridors to the horizon and beyond,
deserts of corporate carpets. Your ankles' sharpness
comforts you in meetings. Your shoe holds
your foot as peel does an apple, restrains the
ground, returns you.

Shoes and torture

we link carelessly: they were bought quickly,
are never right. But step here – a concentration camp,
prisoners forced into shoes sizes too small, suitcases
on their backs, round and round a crazy test bed collage

of rock surfaces all day long, walking and walking,
blisters starting, spreading like a burn around each foot,
all the little bones struggling against each other, the shoes
bulging and bloating, bursting in their effort to be shoes,
soles cracking apart, the body they hold staggering,
staggering, falling to the earth which never stops waiting.

The Burning Tractor

It's stopped at the point where it went up –
the side of the road on the top of Black Lion Hill,
cab and wheels framed by a shining square
of gold heat vibrating across as we edge by

and the fire engine that had bayed its way
through the village traffic ahead of me
now looks much too late and a yellow haired woman
in shorts, with a baby on her hip, is saying,

'Bugger, it's our only bloody tractor too',
while the flames swirl into the already hot afternoon,
upping the temperature to a moment of somewhere else,
Africa, Australia, somewhere incandescent, predatory.

Notes

p 2

The Schoolroom, Temple House: Temple House is an Ascendancy mansion near Tubbercurry, Co.Sligo, Ireland.

p 14

Maggie Philomena: St Philomena was a Roman virgin martyr much revered in the Catholic Church until her name was removed from the Liturgical calendar by the Vatican in 1961.

p 24

The Moon Landing: Sunnyside is a terrace of listed early Victorian houses backing on to Princes Park, Liverpool 8.

p 28

Risotto won a prize in a Times competition in 2009, organised by Alex Renton, for poems about cooking.

p 34

Dickins & Jones: the Regent Street shop which traded in the West End from 1790. It closed in 2006.

p 42

Cy Twombly's Hero and Leandro: refers to the work shown in the Twombly exhibition at Tate Modern in 2008, a polyptych inspired by Marlowe's 'Hero and Leander' and Keats' sonnet 'On a Leander Gem…' both quoted here.

p 43

The Singing Butler: this work (1992) by Scots painter, Jack Vettriano, is, according to many sources, Britain's highest selling reproduced image. The painting itself sold at auction in 2004 for £744,800 – a record for any Scots painting, and for any painting ever sold in Scotland.

p 49

Sachsenhausen: a Nazi prison camp 20 kilometres from Berlin, used from the mid thirties onwards to confine political prisoners.